MW00513066

AIR FRYER RECIPES 2021

EFFORTLESS DELICIOUS APPETIZER RECIPES
FOR BEGINNERS AND ADVANCED USERS

JENNIFER WILSON

Table of Contents

Introduction

Are you always looking for easier and more modern ways to cook the best meals for you and all your loved ones?
Are you constantly searching for useful kitchen appliances that will make your work in the kitchen more fun?
Well, you don't need to search anymore! We present to you today the best kitchen appliance available these days on the market: the air fryer!

Air fryers are simply the best kitchen tools for so many reasons. Are you interested in discovering more about air fryers? Then, pay attention next!

First of all, you need to know that air fryers are special and revolutionary kitchen appliances that cook your food using the circulation of hot air. These tools use a special technology called rapid air technology. Therefore, all the food you cook in these fryers is succulent on the inside and perfectly cooked on the outside.

The next thing you need to find out about air fryers is that they allow you to cook, bake, steam and roast pretty much everything you can imagine.

Last but not least, you should know that air fryers help you cook your meals in a much healthier way.
So many people all over the world just fell in love with this great and amazing tool and now it's your turn to become one of them.

So...long story short, we recommend you to purchase an air fryer right away and to get your hands on this cooking journal as soon as possible!

We can assure you that all the meals you cook in your air fryer will taste so good and that everyone will admire your cooking skills from now one!

So, let's get started!
Have fun cooking with your great air fryer!

Air Fryer Appetizer Recipes

Banana Chips

Preparation time: 10 minutes **Cooking time:** 15 minutes
Servings: 4

Ingredients:

- 4 bananas, peeled and sliced
- A pinch of salt
- ½ teaspoon turmeric powder
- ½ teaspoon chaat masala
- 1 teaspoon olive oil

Directions:

1. In a bowl, mix banana slices with salt, turmeric, chaat masala and oil, toss and leave aside for 10 minutes.
2. Transfer banana slices to your preheated air fryer at 360 degrees F and cook them for 15 minutes flipping them once.
3. Serve as a snack.

Enjoy!

Nutrition: calories 121, fat 1, fiber 2, carbs 3, protein 3

Spring Rolls

Preparation time: 10 minutes **Cooking time:** 25 minutes
Servings: 8

Ingredients:

- 2 cups green cabbage, shredded
- 2 yellow onions, chopped
- 1 carrot, grated
- ½ chili pepper, minced
- 1 tablespoon ginger, grated
- 3 garlic cloves, minced
- 1 teaspoon sugar
- Salt and black pepper to the taste
- 1 teaspoon soy sauce
- 2 tablespoons olive oil
- 10 spring roll sheets
- 2 tablespoons corn flour
- 2 tablespoons water

Directions:

1. Heat up a pan with the oil over medium heat, add cabbage, onions, carrots, chili pepper, ginger, garlic,

sugar, salt, pepper and soy sauce, stir well, cook for 2-3 minutes, take off heat and cool down.

2. Cut spring roll sheets in squares, divide cabbage mix on each and roll them.
3. In a bowl, mix corn flour with water, stir well and seal spring rolls with this mix.
4. Place spring rolls in your air fryer's basket and cook them at 360 degrees F for 10 minutes.
5. Flip roll and cook them for 10 minutes more.
6. Arrange on a platter and serve them as an appetizer.

Enjoy!

Nutrition: calories 214, fat 4, fiber 4, carbs 12, protein 4

Crispy Radish Chips

Preparation time: 10 minutes **Cooking time:** 10 minutes
Servings: 4

Ingredients:

- Cooking spray
- 15 radishes, sliced
- Salt and black pepper to the taste
- 1 tablespoon chives, chopped

Directions:

1. Arrange radish slices in your air fryer's basket, spray them with cooking oil, season with salt and black pepper to the taste, cook them at 350 degrees F for 10 minutes, flipping them halfway, transfer to bowls and serve with chives sprinkled on top.

Enjoy!

Nutrition: calories 80, fat 1, fiber 1, carbs 1, protein 1

Crab Sticks

Preparation time: 10 minutes **Cooking time:** 12 minutes

Servings: 4

Ingredients:

- 10 crabsticks, halved
- 2 teaspoons sesame oil
- 2 teaspoons Cajun seasoning

Directions:

1. Put crab sticks in a bowl, add sesame oil and Cajun seasoning, toss, transfer them to your air fryer's basket and cook at 350 degrees F for 12 minutes.

   Arrange on a platter and serve as an appetizer.

Enjoy!

Nutrition: calories 110, fat 0, fiber 1, carbs 4, protein 2

Air Fried Dill Pickles

Preparation time: 10 minutes **Cooking time:** 5 minutes

Servings: 4

Ingredients:

- 16 ounces jarred dill pickles, cut into wedges and pat dried
- ½ cup white flour
- 1 egg
- ¼ cup milk
- ½ teaspoon garlic powder
- ½ teaspoon sweet paprika
- Cooking spray
- ¼ cup ranch sauce

Directions:

1. In a bowl, combine milk with egg and whisk well.
2. In a second bowl, mix flour with salt, garlic powder and paprika and stir as well
3. Dip pickles in flour, then in egg mix and again in flour and place them in your air fryer.

4. Grease them with cooking spray, cook pickle wedges at 400 degrees F for 5 minutes, transfer to a bowl and serve with ranch sauce on the side.

Enjoy!

Nutrition: calories 109, fat 2, fiber 2, carbs 10, protein 4

Chickpeas Snack

Preparation time: 10 minutes **Cooking time:** 10 minutes
Servings: 4

Ingredients:

- 15 ounces canned chickpeas, drained
- ½ teaspoon cumin, ground
- 1 tablespoon olive oil
- 1 teaspoon smoked paprika
- Salt and black pepper to the taste

Directions:

1. In a bowl, mix chickpeas with oil, cumin, paprika, salt and pepper, toss to coat, place them in your fryer's basket and cook at 390 degrees F for 10 minutes.
2. Divide into bowls and serve as a snack.

Enjoy!

Nutrition: calories 140, fat 1, fiber 6, carbs 20, protein 6

Sausage Balls

Preparation time: 10 minutes **Cooking time:** 15 minutes
Servings: 9

Ingredients:

- 4 ounces sausage meat, ground
- Salt and black pepper to the taste
- 1 teaspoon sage
- ½ teaspoon garlic, minced
- 1 small onion, chopped
- 3 tablespoons breadcrumbs

Directions:

1. In a bowl, mix sausage with salt, pepper, sage, garlic, onion and breadcrumbs, stir well and shape small balls out of this mix.
2. Put them in your air fryer's basket, cook at 360 degrees F for 15 minutes, divide into bowls and serve as a snack.

Enjoy!

Nutrition: calories 130, fat 7, fiber 1, carbs 13, protein 4

Chicken Dip

Preparation time: 10 minutes **Cooking time:** 25 minutes
Servings: 10

Ingredients:

- 3 tablespoons butter, melted
- 1 cup yogurt
- 12 ounces cream cheese
- 2 cups chicken meat, cooked and shredded
- 2 teaspoons curry powder
- 4 scallions, chopped
- 6 ounces Monterey jack cheese, grated
- 1/3 cup raisins
- ¼ cup cilantro, chopped
- ½ cup almonds, sliced
- Salt and black pepper to the taste
- ½ cup chutney

Directions:

1. In a bowl mix cream cheese with yogurt and whisk using your mixer.

2. Add curry powder, scallions, chicken meat, raisins, cheese, cilantro, salt and pepper and stir everything.

3. Spread this into a baking dish that fist your air fryer, sprinkle almonds on top, place in your air fryer, bake at 300 degrees for 25 minutes, divide into bowls, top with chutney and serve as an appetizer.

Enjoy!

Nutrition: calories 240, fat 10, fiber 2, carbs 24, protein 12

Sweet Popcorn

Preparation time: 5 minutes **Cooking time:** 10 minutes

Servings: 4

Ingredients:

- 2 tablespoons corn kernels
- 2 and ½ tablespoons butter
- 2 ounces brown sugar

Directions:

1. Put corn kernels in your air fryer's pan, cook at 400 degrees F for 6 minutes, transfer them to a tray, spread and leave aside for now.
2. Heat up a pan over low heat, add butter, melt it, add sugar and stir until it dissolves.
3. Add popcorn, toss to coat, take off heat and spread on the tray again.
4. Cool down, divide into bowls and serve as a snack.

Enjoy!

Nutrition: calories 70, fat 0.2, fiber 0, carbs 1, protein 1

Apple Chips

Preparation time: 10 minutes **Cooking time:** 10 minutes
Servings: 2

Ingredients:

- 1 apple, cored and sliced
- A pinch of salt
- ½ teaspoon cinnamon powder
- 1 tablespoon white sugar

Directions:

1. In a bowl, mix apple slices with salt, sugar and cinnamon, toss, transfer to your air fryer's basket, cook for 10 minutes at 390 degrees F flipping once.
2. Divide apple chips in bowls and serve as a snack.

Enjoy!

Nutrition: calories 70, fat 0, fiber 4, carbs 3, protein 1

Bread Sticks

Preparation time: 10 minutes **Cooking time:** 10 minutes

Servings: 2

Ingredients:

- 4 bread slices, each cut into 4 sticks
- 2 eggs
- ¼ cup milk
- 1 teaspoon cinnamon powder
- 1 tablespoon honey
- ¼ cup brown sugar
- A pinch of nutmeg

Directions:

1. In a bowl, mix eggs with milk, brown sugar, cinnamon, nutmeg and honey and whisk well.
2. Dip bread sticks in this mix, place them in your air fryer's basket and cook at 360 degrees F for 10 minutes.
3. Divide bread sticks into bowls and serve as a snack.

Enjoy!

Nutrition: calories 140, fat 1, fiber 4, carbs 8, protein 4

Crispy Shrimp

Preparation time: 10 minutes **Cooking time:** 5 minutes
Servings: 4

Ingredients:

- 12 big shrimp, deveined and peeled
- 2 egg whites
- 1 cup coconut, shredded
- 1 cup panko bread crumbs
- 1 cup white flour
- Salt and black pepper to the taste

Directions:

1. In a bowl, mix panko with coconut and stir.
2. Put flour, salt and pepper in a second bowl and whisk egg whites in a third one.
3. Dip shrimp in flour, egg whites mix and coconut, place them all in your air fryer's basket, cook at 350 degrees F for 10 minutes flipping halfway.
4. Arrange on a platter and serve as an appetizer.

Enjoy!

Nutrition: calories 140, fat 4, fiber 0, carbs 3, protein 4

Cajun Shrimp Appetizer

Preparation time: 10 minutes **Cooking time:** 5 minutes
Servings: 2

Ingredients:

- 20 tiger shrimp, peeled and deveined
- Salt and black pepper to the taste
- ½ teaspoon old bay seasoning
- 1 tablespoon olive oil
- ¼ teaspoon smoked paprika

Directions:

1. In a bowl, mix shrimp with oil, salt, pepper, old bay seasoning and paprika and toss to coat.
2. Place shrimp in your air fryer's basket and cook at 390 degrees F for 5 minutes.
3. Arrange them on a platter and serve as an appetizer.

Enjoy!

Nutrition: calories 162, fat 6, fiber 4, carbs 8, protein 14

Crispy Fish Sticks

Preparation time: 10 minutes **Cooking time:** 12 minutes
Servings: 2

Ingredients:

- 4 ounces bread crumbs
- 4 tablespoons olive oil
- 1 egg, whisked
- 4 white fish filets, boneless, skinless and cut into medium sticks
- Salt and black pepper to the taste

Directions:

1. In a bowl, mix bread crumbs with oil and stir well.
2. Put egg in a second bowl, add salt and pepper and whisk well.
3. Dip fish stick in egg and them in bread crumb mix, place them in your air fryer's basket and cook at 360 degrees F for 12 minutes.
4. Arrange fish sticks on a platter and serve as an appetizer.

Enjoy!

Nutrition: calories 160, fat 3, fiber 5, carbs 12, protein 3

Fish Nuggets

Preparation time: 10 minutes **Cooking time:** 12 minutes
Servings: 4

Ingredients:

- 28 ounces fish fillets, skinless and cut into medium pieces
- Salt and black pepper to the taste
- 5 tablespoons flour
- 1 egg, whisked
- 5 tablespoons water
- 3 ounces panko bread crumbs
- 1 tablespoon garlic powder
- 1 tablespoon smoked paprika
- 4 tablespoons homemade mayonnaise
- Lemon juice from ½ lemon
- 1 teaspoon dill, dried
- Cooking spray

Directions:

1. In a bowl, mix flour with water and stir well.
2. Add egg, salt and pepper and whisk well.

3. In a second bowl, mix panko with garlic powder and paprika and stir well.
4. Dip fish pieces in flour and egg mix and then in panko mix, place them in your air fryer's basket, spray them with cooking oil and cook at 400 degrees F for 12 minutes.
5. Meanwhile, in a bowl mix mayo with dill and lemon juice and whisk well.
6. Arrange fish nuggets on a platter and serve with dill mayo on the side.

Enjoy!

Nutrition: calories 332, fat 12, fiber 6, carbs 17, protein 15

Shrimp and Chestnut Rolls

Preparation time: 10 minutes **Cooking time:** 15 minutes
Servings: 4

Ingredients:

- ½ pound already cooked shrimp, chopped
- 8 ounces water chestnuts, chopped
- ½ pounds shiitake mushrooms, chopped
- 2 cups cabbage, chopped
- 2 tablespoons olive oil
- 1 garlic clove, minced
- 1 teaspoon ginger, grated
- 3 scallions, chopped
- Salt and black pepper to the taste
- 1 tablespoon water
- 1 egg yolk
- 6 spring roll wrappers

Directions:

1. Heat up a pan with the oil over medium high heat, add cabbage, shrimp, chestnuts, mushrooms, garlic, ginger, scallions, salt and pepper, stir and cook for 2 minutes.

2. In a bowl, mix egg with water and stir well.

3. Arrange roll wrappers on a working surface, divide shrimp and veggie mix on them, seal edges with egg wash, place them all in your air fryer's basket, cook at 360 degrees F for 15 minutes, transfer to a platter and serve as an appetizer.

Enjoy!

Nutrition: calories 140, fat 3, fiber 1, carbs 12, protein 3

Seafood Appetizer

Preparation time: 10 minutes **Cooking time:** 25 minutes
Servings: 4

Ingredients:

- ½ cup yellow onion, chopped
- 1 cup green bell pepper, chopped
- 1 cup celery, chopped
- 1 cup baby shrimp, peeled and deveined
- 1 cup crabmeat, flaked
- 1 cup homemade mayonnaise
- 1 teaspoon Worcestershire sauce
- Salt and black pepper to the taste
- 2 tablespoons bread crumbs
- 1 tablespoon butter
- 1 teaspoon sweet paprika

Directions:

1. In a bowl, mix shrimp with crab meat, bell pepper, onion, mayo, celery, salt and pepper and stir.
2. Add Worcestershire sauce, stir again and pour everything into a baking dish that fits your air fryer.

3. Sprinkle bread crumbs and add butter, introduce in your air fryer and cook at 320 degrees F for 25 minutes, shaking halfway.
4. Divide into bowl and serve with paprika sprinkled on top as an appetizer.

Enjoy!

Nutrition: calories 200, fat 1, fiber 2, carbs 5, protein 1

Salmon Meatballs

Preparation time: 10 minutes **Cooking time:** 12 minutes
Servings: 4

Ingredients:

- 3 tablespoons cilantro, minced
- 1 pound salmon, skinless and chopped
- 1 small yellow onion, chopped
- 1 egg white
- Salt and black pepper to the taste
- 2 garlic cloves, minced
- ½ teaspoon paprika
- ¼ cup panko
- ½ teaspoon oregano, ground
- Cooking spray

Directions:

1. In your food processor, mix salmon with onion, cilantro, egg white, garlic cloves, salt, pepper, paprika and oregano and stir well.
2. Add panko, blend again and shape meatballs from this mix using your palms.

3. Place them in your air fryer's basket, spray them with cooking spray and cook at 320 degrees F for 12 minutes shaking the fryer halfway.
4. Arrange meatballs on a platter and serve them as an appetizer.

Enjoy!

Nutrition: calories 289, fat 12, fiber 3, carbs 22, protein 23

Easy Chicken Wings

Preparation time: 10 minutes **Cooking time:** 1 hours **Servings:** 2

Ingredients:

- 16 pieces chicken wings
- Salt and black pepper to the taste
- ¼ cup butter
- ¾ cup potato starch
- ¼ cup honey
- 4 tablespoons garlic, minced

Directions:

1. In a bowl, mix chicken wings with salt, pepper and potato starch, toss well, transfer to your air fryer's basket, cook them at 380 degrees F for 25 minutes and at 400 degrees F for 5 minutes more.
2. Meanwhile, heat up a pan with the butter over medium high heat, melt it, add garlic, stir, cook for 5 minutes and then mix with salt, pepper and honey.
3. Whisk well, cook over medium heat for 20 minutes and take off heat.
4. Arrange chicken wings on a platter, drizzle honey sauce all over and serve as an appetizer.

Enjoy!

Nutrition: calories 244, fat 7, fiber 3, carbs 19, protein 8

Chicken Breast Rolls

Preparation time: 10 minutes **Cooking time:** 22 minutes
Servings: 4

Ingredients:

- 2 cups baby spinach
- 4 chicken breasts, boneless and skinless
- 1 cup sun dried tomatoes, chopped
- Salt and black pepper to the taste
- 1 and ½ tablespoons Italian seasoning
- 4 mozzarella slices
- A drizzle of olive oil

Directions:

1. Flatten chicken breasts using a meat tenderizer, divide tomatoes, mozzarella and spinach, season with salt, pepper and Italian seasoning, roll and seal them.
2. Place them in your air fryer's basket, drizzle some oil over them and cook at 375 degrees F for 17 minutes, flipping once.
3. Arrange chicken rolls on a platter and serve them as an appetizer.

Enjoy!

Nutrition: calories 300, fat 1, fiber 4, carbs 7, protein 10

Crispy Chicken Breast Sticks

Preparation time: 10 minutes **Cooking time:** 16 minutes
Servings: 4

Ingredients:

- ¾ cup white flour
- 1 pound chicken breast, skinless, boneless and cut into medium sticks
- 1 teaspoon sweet paprika
- 1 cup panko bread crumbs
- 1 egg, whisked
- Salt and black pepper to the taste
- ½ tablespoon olive oil
- Zest from 1 lemon, grated

Directions:

1. In a bowl, mix paprika with flour, salt, pepper and lemon zest and stir.
2. Put whisked egg in another bowl and the panko breadcrumbs in a third one.
3. Dredge chicken pieces in flour, egg and panko and place them in your lined air fryer's basket, drizzle the oil over them, cook at 400 degrees F for 8 minutes, flip and cook for 8 more minutes.
4. Arrange them on a platter and serve as a snack.

Enjoy!

Nutrition: calories 254, fat 4, fiber 7, carbs 20, protein 22

Beef Roll s

Preparation time: 10 minutes **Cooking time:** 14 minutes

Servings: 4

Ingredients:

- 2 pounds beef steak, opened and flattened with a meat tenderizer
- Salt and black pepper to the taste
- 1 cup baby spinach
- 3 ounces red bell pepper, roasted and chopped
- 6 slices provolone cheese
- 3 tablespoons pesto

Directions:

1. Arrange flattened beef steak on a cutting board, spread pesto all over, add cheese in a single layer, add bell peppers, spinach, salt and pepper to the taste.
2. Roll your steak, secure with toothpicks, season again with salt and pepper, place roll in your air fryer's basket and cook at 400 degrees F for 14 minutes, rotating roll halfway.
3. Leave aside to cool down, cut into 2 inch smaller rolls, arrange on a platter and serve them as an appetizer.

Enjoy!

Nutrition: calories 230, fat 1, fiber 3, carbs 12, protein 10

Empanadas

Preparation time: 10 minutes **Cooking time:** 25 minutes

Servings: 4

Ingredients:

- 1 package empanada shells
- 1 tablespoon olive oil
- 1 pound beef meat, ground
- 1 yellow onion, chopped
- Salt and black pepper to the taste
- 2 garlic cloves, minced
- ½ teaspoon cumin, ground
- ¼ cup tomato salsa
- 1 egg yolk whisked with 1 tablespoon water
- 1 green bell pepper, chopped

Directions:

1. Heat up a pan with the oil over medium high heat, add beef and brown on all sides.
2. Add onion, garlic, salt, pepper, bell pepper and tomato salsa, stir and cook for 15 minutes.

3. Divide cooked meat in empanada shells, brush them with egg wash and seal.
4. Place them in your air fryer's steamer basket and cook at 350 degrees F for 10 minutes.
5. Arrange on a platter and serve as an appetizer.

Enjoy!

Nutrition: calories 274, fat 17, fiber 14, carbs 20, protein 7

Greek Lamb Meatballs

Preparation time: 10 minutes **Cooking time:** 8 minutes
Servings: 10

Ingredients:

- 4 ounces lamb meat, minced
- Salt and black pepper to the taste
- 1 slice of bread, toasted and crumbled
- 2 tablespoons feta cheese, crumbled
- ½ tablespoon lemon peel, grated
- 1 tablespoon oregano, chopped

Directions:

1. In a bowl, combine meat with bread crumbs, salt, pepper, feta, oregano and lemon peel, stir well, shape 10 meatballs and place them in you air fryer.
2. Cook at 400 degrees F for 8 minutes, arrange them on a platter and serve as an appetizer.

Enjoy!

Nutrition: calories 234, fat 12, fiber 2, carbs 20, protein 30

Beef Party Rolls

Preparation time: 10 minutes **Cooking time:** 15 minutes
Servings: 4

Ingredients:

- 14 ounces beef stock
- 7 ounces white wine
- 4 beef cutlets
- Salt and black pepper to the taste
- 8 sage leaves
- 4 ham slices
- 1 tablespoon butter, melted

Directions:

1. Heat up a pan with the stock over medium high heat, add wine, cook until it reduces, take off heat and divide into small bowls
2. Season cutlets with salt and pepper, cover with sage and roll each in ham slices.
3. Brush rolls with butter, place them in your air fryer's basket and cook at 400 degrees F for 15 minutes.

4. Arrange rolls on a platter and serve them with the gravy on the side.

Enjoy!

Nutrition: calories 260, fat 12, fiber 1, carbs 22, protein 21

Pork Rolls

Preparation time: 10 minutes **Cooking time:** 40 minutes

Servings: 4

Ingredients:

- 1 15 ounces pork fillet
- ½ teaspoon chili powder
- 1 teaspoon cinnamon powder
- 1 garlic clove, minced
- Salt and black pepper to the taste
- 2 tablespoons olive oil
- 1 and ½ teaspoon cumin, ground
- 1 red onion, chopped
- 3 tablespoons parsley, chopped

Directions:

1. In a bowl, mix cinnamon with garlic, salt, pepper, chili powder, oil, onion, parsley and cumin and stir well
2. Put pork fillet on a cutting board, flatten it using a meat tenderizer. And use a meat tenderizer to flatten it.

3. Spread onion mix on pork, roll tight, cut into medium rolls, place them in your preheated air fryer at 360 degrees F and cook them for 35 minutes.
4. Arrange them on a platter and serve as an appetizer

Enjoy!

Nutrition: calories 304, fat 12, fiber 1, carbs 15, protein 23

Beef Patties

Preparation time: 10 minutes **Cooking time:** 8 minutes

Servings: 4

Ingredients:

- 14 ounces beef, minced
- 2 tablespoons ham, cut into strips
- 1 leek, chopped
- 3 tablespoons bread crumbs
- Salt and black pepper to the taste
- ½ teaspoon nutmeg, ground

Directions:

1. In a bowl, mix beef with leek, salt, pepper, ham, breadcrumbs and nutmeg, stir well and shape small patties out of this mix.
2. Place them in your air fryer's basket, cook at 400 degrees F for 8 minutes, arrange on a platter and serve as an appetizer.

Enjoy!

Nutrition: calories 260, fat 12, fiber 3, carbs 12, protein 21

Roasted Bell Pepper Rolls

Preparation time: 10 minutes **Cooking time:** 10 minutes
Servings: 8

Ingredients:

- 1 yellow bell pepper, halved
- 1 orange bell pepper, halved
- Salt and black pepper to the taste
- 4 ounces feta cheese, crumbled
- 1 green onion, chopped
- 2 tablespoons oregano, chopped

Directions:

1. In a bowl, mix cheese with onion, oregano, salt and pepper and whisk well.
2. Place bell pepper halves in your air fryer's basket, cook at 400 degrees F for 10 minutes, transfer to a cutting board, cool down and peel.
3. Divide cheese mix on each bell pepper half, roll, secure with toothpicks, arrange on a platter and serve as an appetizer.

Enjoy!

Nutrition: calories 170, fat 1, fiber 2, carbs 8, protein 5

Stuffed Peppers

Preparation time: 10 minutes **Cooking time:** 8 minutes
Servings: 8

Ingredients:

- 8 small bell peppers, tops cut off and seeds removed
- 1 tablespoon olive oil
- Salt and black pepper to the taste
- 3.5 ounces goat cheese, cut into 8 pieces

Directions:

1. In a bowl, mix cheese with oil with salt and pepper and toss to coat.
2. Stuff each pepper with goat cheese, place them in your air fryer's basket, cook at 400 degrees F for 8 minutes, arrange on a platter and serve as an appetizer.

Enjoy!

Nutrition: calories 120, fat 1, fiber 1, carbs 12, protein 8

Herbed Tomatoes Appetizer

Preparation time: 10 minutes **Cooking time:** 20 minutes
Servings: 2

Ingredients:

- 2 tomatoes, halved
- Cooking spray
- Salt and black pepper to the taste
- 1 teaspoon parsley, dried
- 1 teaspoon basil, dried
- 1 teaspoon oregano, dried
- 1 teaspoon rosemary, dried

Directions:

1. Spray tomato halves with cooking oil, season with salt, pepper, parsley, basil, oregano and rosemary over them.
2. Place them in your air fryer's basket and cook at 320 degrees F for 20 minutes.
3. Arrange them on a platter and serve as an appetizer.

Enjoy!

Nutrition: calories 100, fat 1, fiber 1, carbs 4, protein 1

Olives Balls

Preparation time: 10 minutes **Cooking time:** 4 minutes
Servings: 6

Ingredients:

- 8 black olives, pitted and minced
- Salt and black pepper to the taste
- 2 tablespoons sun dried tomato pesto
- 14 pepperoni slices, chopped
- 4 ounces cream cheese
- 1 tablespoons basil, chopped

Directions:

1. In a bowl, mix cream cheese with salt, pepper, basil, pepperoni, pesto and black olives, stir well and shape small balls out of this mix.
2. Place them in your air fryer's basket, cook at 350 degrees F for 4 minutes, arrange on a platter and serve as a snack.

Enjoy!

Nutrition: calories 100, fat 1, fiber 0, carbs 8, protein 3

Jalapeno Balls

Preparation time: 10 minutes **Cooking time:** 4 minutes **Servings:** 3

Ingredients:

- 3 bacon slices, cooked and crumbled
- 3 ounces cream cheese
- ¼ teaspoon onion powder
- Salt and black pepper to the taste
- 1 jalapeno pepper, chopped
- ½ teaspoon parsley, dried
- ¼ teaspoon garlic powder

Directions:

1. In a bowl, mix cream cheese with jalapeno pepper, onion and garlic powder, parsley, bacon salt and pepper and stir well.
2. Shape small balls out of this mix, place them in your air fryer's basket, cook at 350 degrees F for 4 minutes, arrange on a platter and serve as an appetizer.

Enjoy!

Nutrition: calories 172, fat 4, fiber 1, carbs 12, protein 5

Wrapped Shrimp

Preparation time: 10 minutes **Cooking time:** 8 minutes **Servings:** 16

Ingredients:

- 2 tablespoons olive oil
- 10 ounces already cooked shrimp, peeled and deveined
- 1 tablespoons mint, chopped
- 1/3 cup blackberries, ground
- 11 prosciutto sliced
- 1/3 cup red wine

Directions:

1. Wrap each shrimp in a prosciutto slices, drizzle the oil over them, rub well, place in your preheated air fryer at 390 degrees F and fry them for 8 minutes.
2. Meanwhile, heat up a pan with ground blackberries over medium heat, add mint and wine, stir, cook for 3 minutes and take off heat.
3. Arrange shrimp on a platter, drizzle blackberries sauce over them and serve as an appetizer.

Enjoy!

Nutrition: calories 224, fat 12, fiber 2, carbs 12, protein 14

Broccoli Patties

Preparation time: 10 minutes **Cooking time:** 10 minutes
Servings: 12

Ingredients:

- 4 cups broccoli florets
- 1 and ½ cup almond flour
- 1 teaspoon paprika
- Salt and black pepper to the taste
- 2 eggs
- ¼ cup olive oil
- 2 cups cheddar cheese, grated
- 1 teaspoon garlic powder
- ½ teaspoon apple cider vinegar
- ½ teaspoon baking soda

Directions:

1. Put broccoli florets in your food processor, add salt and pepper, blend well and transfer to a bowl.
2. Add almond flour, salt, pepper, paprika, garlic powder, baking soda, cheese, oil, eggs and vinegar, stir well and shape 12 patties out of this mix.

3. Place them in your preheated air fryer's basket and cook at 350 degrees F for 10 minutes.
4. Arrange patties on a platter and serve as an appetizer.

Enjoy!

Nutrition: calories 203, fat 12, fiber 2, carbs 14, protein 2

Different Stuffed Peppers

Preparation time: 10 minutes **Cooking time:** 20 minutes

Servings: 6

Ingredients:

- 1 pound mini bell peppers, halved
- Salt and black pepper to the taste
- 1 teaspoon garlic powder
- 1 teaspoon sweet paprika
- ½ teaspoon oregano, dried
- ¼ teaspoon red pepper flakes
- 1 pound beef meat, ground
- 1 and ½ cups cheddar cheese, shredded
- 1 tablespoons chili powder
- 1 teaspoon cumin, ground
- Sour cream for serving

Directions:

1. In a bowl, mix chili powder with paprika, salt, pepper, cumin, oregano, pepper flakes and garlic powder and stir.

2. Heat up a pan over medium heat, add beef, stir and brown for 10 minutes.
3. Add chili powder mix, stir, take off heat and stuff pepper halves with this mix.
4. Sprinkle cheese all over, place peppers in your air fryer's basket and cook them at 350 degrees F for 6 minutes.
5. Arrange peppers on a platter and serve them with sour cream on the side.

Enjoy!

Nutrition: calories 170, fat 22, fiber 3, carbs 6, protein 27

Cheesy Zucchini Snack

Preparation time: 10 minutes **Cooking time:** 8 minutes **Servings:** 4

Ingredients:

- 1 cup mozzarella, shredded
- ¼ cup tomato sauce
- 1 zucchini, sliced
- Salt and black pepper to the taste
- A pinch of cumin
- Cooking spray

Directions:

1. Arrange zucchini slices in your air fryer's basket, spray them with cooking oil, spread tomato sauce all over, them, season with salt, pepper, cumin, sprinkle mozzarella at the end and cook them at 320 degrees F for 8 minutes.
2. Arrange them on a platter and serve as a snack.

Enjoy!

Nutrition: calories 150, fat 4, fiber 2, carbs 12, protein 4

Spinach Balls

Preparation time: 10 minutes **Cooking time:** 7 minutes **Servings:** 30

Ingredients:

- 4 tablespoons butter, melted
- 2 eggs
- 1 cup flour
- 16 ounces spinach
- 1/3 cup feta cheese, crumbled
- ¼ teaspoon nutmeg, ground
- 1/3 cup parmesan, grated
- Salt and black pepper to the taste
- 1 tablespoon onion powder
- 3 tablespoons whipping cream
- 1 teaspoon garlic powder

Directions:

1. In your blender, mix spinach with butter, eggs, flour, feta cheese, parmesan, nutmeg, whipping cream, salt, pepper, onion and garlic pepper, blend very well and keep in the freezer for 10 minutes.

2. Shape 30 spinach balls, place them in your air fryer's basket and cook at 300 degrees F for 7 minutes.
3. Serve as a party appetizer.

Enjoy!

Nutrition: calories 60, fat 5, fiber 1, carbs 1, protein 2

Mushrooms Appetizer

Preparation time: 10 minutes **Cooking time:** 10 minutes
Servings: 4

Ingredients:

- ¼ cup mayonnaise
- 1 teaspoon garlic powder
- 1 small yellow onion, chopped
- 24 ounces white mushroom caps
- Salt and black pepper to the taste
- 1 teaspoon curry powder
- 4 ounces cream cheese, soft
- ¼ cup sour cream
- ½ cup Mexican cheese, shredded
- 1 cup shrimp, cooked, peeled, deveined and chopped

Directions:

1. In a bowl, mix mayo with garlic powder, onion, curry powder, cream cheese, sour cream, Mexican cheese, shrimp, salt and pepper to the taste and whisk well.

2. Stuff mushrooms with this mix, place them in your air fryer's basket and cook at 300 degrees F for 10 minutes.
3. Arrange on a platter and serve as an appetizer.

Enjoy!

Nutrition: calories 200, fat 20, fiber 3, carbs 16, protein 14

Cheesy Party Wings

Preparation time: 10 minutes **Cooking time:** 12 minutes

Servings: 6

Ingredients:

- 6 pound chicken wings, halved
- Salt and black pepper to the taste
- ½ teaspoon Italian seasoning
- 2 tablespoons butter
- ½ cup parmesan cheese, grated
- A pinch of red pepper flakes, crushed
- 1 teaspoon garlic powder
- 1 egg

Directions:

1. Arrange chicken wings in your air fryer's basket and cook at 390 degrees F and cook for 9 minutes.
2. Meanwhile, in your blender, mix butter with cheese, egg, salt, pepper, pepper flakes, garlic powder and Italian seasoning and blend very well.

3. Take chicken wings out, pour cheese sauce over them, toss to coat well and cook in your air fryer's basket at 390 degrees F for 3 minutes.
4. Serve them as an appetizer.

Enjoy!

Nutrition: calories 204, fat 8, fiber 1, carbs 18, protein 14

Cheese Sticks

Preparation time: 1 hour and 10 minutes **Cooking time:** 8 minutes **Servings:** 16

Ingredients:

- 2 eggs, whisked
- Salt and black pepper to the taste
- 8 mozzarella cheese strings, cut into halves
- 1 cup parmesan, grated
- 1 tablespoon Italian seasoning
- Cooking spray
- 1 garlic clove, minced

Directions:

1. In a bowl, mix parmesan with salt, pepper, Italian seasoning and garlic and stir well.
2. Put whisked eggs in another bowl.
3. Dip mozzarella sticks in egg mixture, then in cheese mix.
4. Dip them again in egg and in parmesan mix and keep them in the freezer for 1 hour.

5. Spray cheese sticks with cooking oil, place them in your air fryer's basket and cook at 390 degrees F for 8 minutes flipping them halfway.

6. Arrange them on a platter and serve as an appetizer.

Enjoy!

Nutrition: calories 140, fat 5, fiber 1, carbs 3, protein 4

Sweet Bacon Snack

Preparation time: 10 minutes **Cooking time:** 30 minutes
Servings: 16

Ingredients:

- ½ teaspoon cinnamon powder
- 16 bacon slices
- 1 tablespoon avocado oil
- 3 ounces dark chocolate
- 1 teaspoon maple extract

Directions:

1. Arrange bacon slices in your air fryer's basket, sprinkle cinnamon mix over them and cook them at 300 degrees F for 30 minutes.
2. Heat up a pot with the oil over medium heat, add chocolate and stir until it melts.
3. Add maple extract, stir, take off heat and leave aside to cool down a bit.
4. Take bacon strips out of the oven, leave them to cool down, dip each in chocolate mix, place them on a

parchment paper and leave them to cool down completely.

5. Serve cold as a snack.

Enjoy!

Nutrition: calories 200, fat 4, fiber 5, carbs 12, protein 3

Chicken Rolls

Preparation time: 2 hours and 10 minutes **Cooking time:** 10 minutes **Servings:** 12

Ingredients:

- 4 ounces blue cheese, crumbled
- 2 cups chicken, cooked and chopped
- Salt and black pepper to the taste
- 2 green onions, chopped
- 2 celery stalks, finely chopped
- ½ cup tomato sauce
- 12 egg roll wrappers
- Cooking spray

Directions:

1. In a bowl, mix chicken meat with blue cheese, salt, pepper, green onions, celery and tomato sauce, stir well and keep in the fridge for 2 hours.
2. Place egg wrappers on a working surface, divide chicken mix on them, roll and seal edges.

3. Place rolls in your air fryer's basket, spray them with cooking oil and cook at 350 degrees F for 10 minutes, flipping them halfway.

Enjoy!

Nutrition: calories 220, fat 7, fiber 2, carbs 14, protein 10

Tasty Kale and Celery Crackers

Preparation time: 10 minutes **Cooking time:** 20 minutes

Servings: 6

Ingredients:

- 2 cups flax seed, ground
- 2 cups flax seed, soaked overnight and drained
- 4 bunches kale, chopped
- 1 bunch basil, chopped
- ½ bunch celery, chopped
- 4 garlic cloves, minced
- 1/3 cup olive oil

Directions:

1. In your food processor mix ground flaxseed with celery, kale, basil and garlic and blend well.
2. Add oil and soaked flaxseed and blend again, spread in your air fryer's pan, cut into medium crackers and cook them at 380 degrees F for 20 minutes.
3. Divide into bowls and serve as an appetizer.

Enjoy!

Nutrition: calories 143, fat 1, fiber 2, carbs 8, protein 4

Egg White Chips

Preparation time: 5 minutes **Cooking time:** 8 minutes **Servings:** 2

Ingredients:
- ½ tablespoon water
- 2 tablespoons parmesan, shredded
- 4 eggs whites
- Salt and black pepper to the taste

Directions:
1. In a bowl, mix egg whites with salt, pepper and water and whisk well.
2. Spoon this into a muffin pan that fits your air fryer, sprinkle cheese on top, introduce in your air fryer and cook at 350 degrees F for 8 minutes.
3. Arrange egg white chips on a platter and serve as a snack.

Enjoy!

Nutrition: calories 180, fat 2, fiber 1, carbs 12, protein 7

Tuna Cakes

Preparation time: 10 minutes **Cooking time:** 10 minutes
Servings: 12

Ingredients:

- 15 ounces canned tuna, drain and flaked
- 3 eggs
- ½ teaspoon dill, dried
- 1 teaspoon parsley, dried
- ½ cup red onion, chopped
- 1 teaspoon garlic powder
- Salt and black pepper to the taste
- Cooking spray

Directions:

1. In a bowl, mix tuna with salt, pepper, dill, parsley, onion, garlic powder and eggs, stir well and shape medium cakes out of this mix.
2. Place tuna cakes in your air fryer's basket, spray them with cooking oil and cook at 350 degrees F for 10 minutes, flipping them halfway.
3. Arrange them on a platter and serve as an appetizer.

Enjoy!

Nutrition: calories 140, fat 2, fiber 1, carbs 8, protein 6

Calamari and Shrimp Snack

Preparation time: 10 minutes **Cooking time:** 20 minutes
Servings: 1

Ingredients:

- 8 ounces calamari, cut into medium rings
- 7 ounces shrimp, peeled and deveined
- 1 eggs
- 3 tablespoons white flour
- 1 tablespoon olive oil
- 2 tablespoons avocado, chopped
- 1 teaspoon tomato paste
- 1 tablespoon mayonnaise
- A splash of Worcestershire sauce
- 1 teaspoon lemon juice
- Salt and black pepper to the taste
- ½ teaspoon turmeric powder

Directions:

1. In a bowl, whisk egg with oil, add calamari rings and shrimp and toss to coat.

2. In another bowl, mix flour with salt, pepper and turmeric and stir.
3. Dredge calamari and shrimp in this mix, place them in your air fryer's basket and cook at 350 degrees F for 9 minutes, flipping them once.
4. Meanwhile, in a bowl, mix avocado with mayo and tomato paste and mash using a fork.
5. Add Worcestershire sauce, lemon juice, salt and pepper and stir well.
6. Arrange calamari and shrimp on a platter and serve with the sauce on the side.

Enjoy!

Nutrition: calories 288, fat 23, fiber 3, carbs 10, protein 15

Cauliflower Cakes

Preparation time: 10 minutes **Cooking time:** 10 minutes

Servings: 6

Ingredients:

- 3 and ½ cups cauliflower rice
- 2 eggs
- ¼ cup white flour
- ½ cup parmesan, grated
- Salt and black pepper to the taste
- Cooking spray

Directions:

1. In a bowl, mix cauliflower rice with salt and pepper, stir and squeeze excess water.
2. Transfer cauliflower to another bowl, add eggs, salt, pepper, flour and parmesan, stir really well and shape your cakes.
3. Grease your air fryer with cooking spray, heat it up at 400 degrees, add cauliflower cakes and cook them for 10 minutes flipping them halfway.
4. Divide cakes on plates and serve as a side dish.

Enjoy!

Nutrition: calories 125, fat 2, fiber 6, carbs 8, protein 3

Creamy Brussels Sprouts

Preparation time: 10 minutes **Cooking time:** 25 minutes
Servings: 8

Ingredients:

- 3 pounds Brussels sprouts, halved
- A drizzle of olive oil
- 1 pound bacon, chopped
- Salt and black pepper to the taste
- 4 tablespoons butter
- 3 shallots, chopped
- 1 cup milk
- 2 cups heavy cream
- ¼ teaspoon nutmeg, ground
- 3 tablespoons prepared horseradish

Directions:

1. Preheated you air fryer at 370 degrees F, add oil, bacon, salt and pepper and Brussels sprouts and toss.
2. Add butter, shallots, heavy cream, milk, nutmeg and horseradish, toss again and cook for 25 minutes.
3. Divide among plates and serve as a side dish.

Enjoy!

Nutrition: calories 214, fat 5, fiber 8, carbs 12, protein 5

Cheddar Biscuits

Preparation time: 10 minutes **Cooking time:** 20 minutes
Servings: 8

Ingredients:

- 2 and 1/3 cup self-rising flour
- ½ cup butter+ 1 tablespoon, melted
- 2 tablespoons sugar
- ½ cup cheddar cheese, grated
- 1 and 1/3 cup buttermilk
- 1 cup flour

Directions:

1. In a bowl, mix self-rising flour with ½ cup butter, sugar, cheddar cheese and buttermilk and stir until you obtain a dough.
2. Spread 1 cup flour on a working surface, roll dough, flatten it, cut 8 circles with a cookie cutter and coat them with flour.
3. Line your air fryer's basket with tin foil, add biscuits, brush them with melted butter and cook them at 380 degrees F for 20 minutes.
4. Divide among plates and serve as a side.

Enjoy!

Nutrition: calories 221, fat 3, fiber 8, carbs 12, protein 4

Zucchini Fries

Preparation time: 10 minutes **Cooking time:** 12 minutes

Servings: 4

Ingredients:

- 1 zucchini, cut into medium sticks
- A drizzle of olive oil
- Salt and black pepper to the taste
- 2 eggs, whisked
- 1 cup bread crumbs
- ½ cup flour

Directions:

1. Put flour in a bowl and mix with salt and pepper and stir.
2. Put breadcrumbs in another bowl.
3. In a third bowl mix eggs with a pinch of salt and pepper.
4. Dredge zucchini fries in flour, then in eggs and in bread crumbs at the end.

5. Grease your air fryer with some olive oil, heat up at 400 degrees F, add zucchini fries and cook them for 12 minutes.
6. Serve them as a side dish.

Enjoy!

Nutrition: calories 172, fat 3, fiber 3, carbs 7, protein 3

Conclusion

Air frying is one of the most popular cooking methods these days and air fryers have become one of the most amazing tools in the kitchen.

Air fryers help you cook healthy and delicious meals in no time! You don't need to be an expert in the kitchen in order to cook special dishes for you and your loved ones!

You just have to own an air fryer and this great air fryer cookbook!

You will soon make the best dishes ever and you will impress everyone around you with your home cooked meals!

Just trust us! Get your hands on an air fryer and on this useful air fryer recipes collection and start your new cooking experience! Have fun!

CPSIA information can be obtained
at www.ICGtesting.com
Printed in the USA
BVHW040714220321
603170BV00004B/797